Note to Parents and Teachers

The READING ABOUT: STARTERS series introduces key science vocabulary to young children while encouraging them to discover and understand the world around them. The series works as a set of graded readers in three levels.

LEVEL 1: BEGINNING TO READ follows guidelines set out in the National Curriculum for Year 1. These books can be read alone or as part of guided or group reading. Each book has three sections:

• Information pages that introduce new words. These key words appear in bold throughout the book for easy recognition.
• A lively story that recalls this vocabulary and encourages children to use these words when they talk and write.
• A quiz and word search ask children to look back and recall what they have read.

MAKE A NOISE looks at SOUND AND HEARING. Below are some activities related to the questions on the information spreads that parents, carers and teachers can use to discuss and develop further ideas and concepts:

p. 5 *What sounds or noises don't you like? Why?* Ask children to think about why certain noises are annoying – whining noises, very loud noises, shouting etc. Could be linked to a "listening walk", or a sound quiz using recorded sounds on tape/CD/computer.

p. 7 *Sit close to a sound. Then sit far away. Does it sound any different?* Ask children to think about sounds they hear from far away, e.g. thunder/bells, and what it is like to be near a very loud sound. Could also mention that loud music can damage their ears.

p. 9 *Can you make high and low sounds?* E.g. whistling, growling.

p. 11 *What other sounds does your voice make?* Ask children to think about how they make sounds with lips, tongue, throat, nose: e.g. hiss, boo, hum, raspberry, cough, snore!

p. 13 *Can you sound like an instrument with your voice?* Ask children to make noise like a trumpet/drum/guitar – doing actions if they know them. You could also listen to CDs/video clips to learn about sounds made by individual instruments.

p. 15 *Does the sound change if you stretch a rubber band?* Could also look at how other instruments create high and low notes, e.g. holes on recorder, strings inside piano.

p. 17 *What other animals have big ears?* Ask children to think about why good hearing is important for both hunters and prey, e.g. foxes and rabbits.

p. 21 *Why should you stop, look and listen when you cross the road?* If possible, show children a video about road safety and ask why hearing is important for safety.

ADVISORY TEAM

Educational Consultant
Andrea Bright – Science Co-ordinator, Trafalgar Junior School, Twickenham

Literacy Consultant
Jackie Holderness – former Senior Lecturer in Primary Education, Westminster Institute, Oxford Brookes University

Series Consultants
Anne Fussell – Early Years Teacher and University Tutor, Westminster College, Oxford Brookes University

David Fussell – C.Chem., FRSC

CONTENTS

© Aladdin Books Ltd 2004

Designed and produced by
Aladdin Books Ltd
2/3 Fitzroy Mews
London W1T 6DF

First published in
Great Britain in 2004 by
Franklin Watts
96 Leonard Street
London EC2A 4XD

A catalogue record for this book is available from the British Library.

ISBN 0 7496 5594 1

Printed in UAE

Editor: Sally Hewitt

Design: Simon Morse; Flick, Book Design and Graphics

Picture research:
Brian Hunter Smart

Thanks to:
• The pupils of Trafalgar Infants School, Twickenham for appearing as models in this book.
• Lynne Thompson for helping to organise the photoshoots.
• The pupils and teachers of Trafalgar Junior School, Twickenham and St. Nicholas C.E. Infant School, Wallingford, for testing the sample books.

Photocredits
Abbreviations: l-left, r-right, b-bottom, t-top, c-centre, m-middle
Front cover tl, tr & b, 2tl, 2bl, 3, 7r, 8, 9, 11b, 13 all, 14t, 15, 16br, 17br, 18b, 19tl, 19tr, 20, 21tr, 25tl, 25bl, 26tl, 29tl, 30tr, 31ml, 32ml, 32mrt, 32bl — PBD. Front cover tc — Corbis. 2ml, 6, 24bl, 32tr — Digital Stock. 4, 22, 32br — Corel. 5, 19bl, 23tr, 29b, 32tl — Select Pictures. 7l, 27br, 32mlt — Comstock. 10, 16t, 26br, 31tr, 32mr — Brand X Pictures. 11tr, 23b — Photodisc. 12 all, 14bl, 31mr, 32mlb — Stockbyte. 17t, 32mrb — John Foxx Images. 19br, 21ml, 21br, 24tr, 25mr, 28bl, 31bl — Jim Pipe. 27tl — Scott Bauer/USDA. 28tr — Simon Morse.

SOUND AND HEARING

Make a Noise!

by Jim Pipe

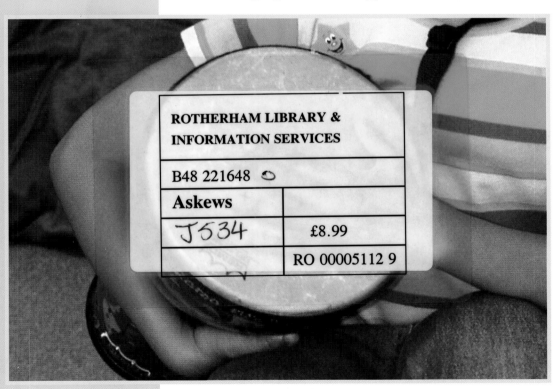

Aladdin/Watts
London • Sydney

Sit and listen.

What **sounds** can you hear?

Some **sounds** are nice,

like the **sound** of water.

4

Some **sounds** are not so nice.

This saw makes a loud **sound**.
It makes a lot of **noise**.

• What sounds or noises don't you like? Why?

Some sounds are **loud**.

When a lion roars, it is very **loud**.

You can hear a **loud** sound far away.

6

Some noises are **quiet**.

When a mouse moves, it is very **quiet**.
You must be close to hear it.

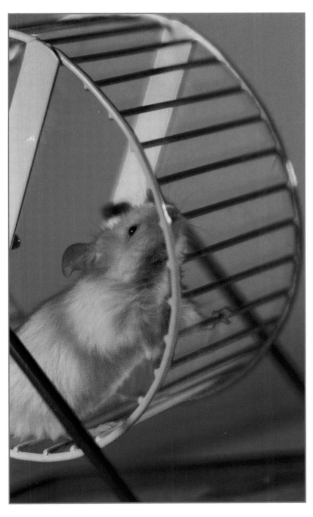

• Sit close to a sound. Then sit far away.
Is there any difference?

Some sounds are **high**.

A whistle makes a **high** sound.

So does a mouse!

We say it squeaks.

Some sounds are **low**.
A big drum makes a **low** sound.
It makes a noise like boom, boom!

• Can you make high and low sounds?

Your **voice** makes lots of sounds.
You use your **voice** to **talk**.

If you **talk** loudly, you **shout**.
If you **talk** quietly, you **whisper**.

You use your **voice** to **sing** or laugh.

When you **sing**, you make high sounds and low sounds.

• What other sounds does your voice make?

Instruments make high and low sounds. How do you play these **instruments**?

Recorder

Drum

Tambourine

You **bang** a drum.

You **rattle** a tambourine.

You **blow** into a recorder.
It goes toot, toot!

• Can you sound like an instrument with your voice?

You **pluck** a guitar.
You pull the strings
with your fingers.

You can make high
sounds and low sounds.

14

You can **pluck** a rubber band too.
Your finger pulls the rubber band.
You make it **buzz**.

• *Does the sound change if you stretch a rubber band?*

You **hear** when
sounds go into
your **ears**.

Cover your **ears**. It is hard to **hear!**

16

This zebra has big **ears**.
Animals with big **ears hear** well.

Make your **ears** bigger.
Put a hand behind
your **ear**.
Can you **hear** better?

• What other animals have big ears?

Ears tell you where a sound comes from, its **direction**.

Go outside and **listen** for sounds. Where are they coming from?

18

Shut your eyes.

Ask a friend to make a noise. **Listen**.

Can you point in his or her **direction**?

What is your friend doing?

Knocking

Whistling

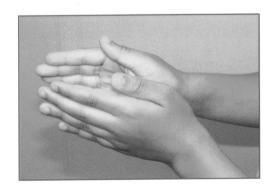

Clapping

Munching!

• What sounds can you hear at night?

A noise far away is **quieter**.
A noise close by is **louder**.

Ask a friend to walk away from you.
Do their footsteps get **louder**?

20

When you cross
the road stop,
look and listen.

When a car
comes closer,
it gets **louder**.

When a car
drives away,
it gets **quieter**.

• Why should you stop, look and listen
when you cross the road?

Some sounds make you feel happy or sad. Does **music** make you happy?

Music can make you **dance** or sing.

22

Some sounds warn us.
An **alarm** clock tells
you to get up.

A noisy **siren** tells you
an ambulance is in a hurry.

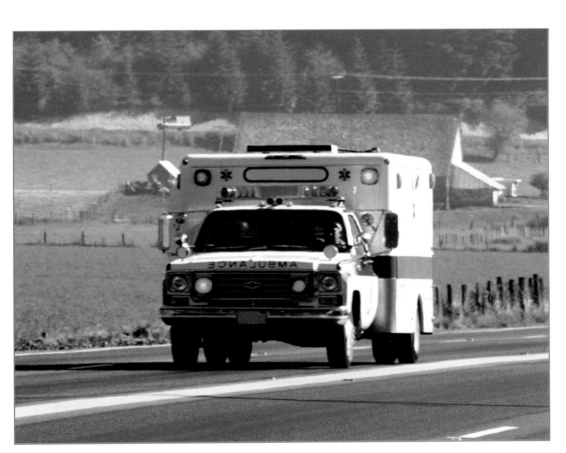

• What warning sounds do you hear at school?

Beep! Beep! Beep!

What's that **noise**?

It is my **alarm** clock.
It tells me that it is time to get up.

I am busy today. I want to paint.

I will find a **quiet** room.

24

La! La! La!

What's that **noise**?

I **hear music**.
It is the radio.

Dad **sings** along.
He has a **low voice**.

When he is happy,
Dad whistles too.
It makes a
high noise.

Oh no!
It is too **noisy** here!

25

Ring! Ring!

What's that **noise**?

It's the telephone.
My sister starts
to **talk**.

She laughs and **shouts**
and **whispers**.
I say, "Shhhhh!"
She does not **hear**.

Grrr! It is too
noisy here!

I go into the garden.

Buzz! Buzz!

What's that **noise**?

A bee **buzzes** by.
It is a **quiet sound**.

Woof! Woof!

What's that **noise**?
A dog barks next door.
Its bark is very **loud**.

Hmmph. It is too
noisy here!

27

I look into
the shed.

Bang!
Bang!
Bang!

What's that **noise**?
It is very **loud**.

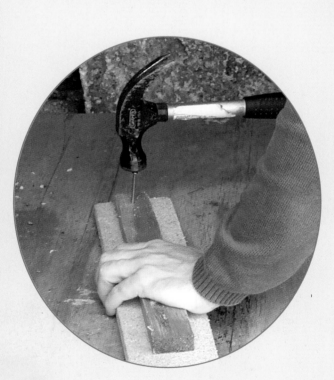

My big brother
is **banging** a nail
with a hammer.

It is too
noisy here.

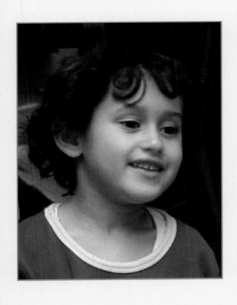

I sit by the front door.

Wee-ooh!
Wee-ooh!
Wee-ooh!

What's that **noise**?

It is a **siren**.
The **noise** gets **louder** and **louder**.
A fire engine rushes by.
I put my hands over my **ears**.

Coo-ee! Nadia!

What's that **noise**?
My friend Mary
is calling me.

"Let's play some **music**," says Mary.
We go inside. I shake a shaker.
Mary **rattles** a tambourine.

We can be **noisy** too!

Listen for a minute. Draw pictures of all the things you **hear**.

Or draw a picture of an animal. Write down the **sounds** that it makes.

Neigh!

Clip-clop

QUIZ

How do you **talk** very **quietly**?

Answer on page 10

What **instrument** do you **blow**?

Answer on page 13

How do you **pluck** a guitar?

Answer on page 14

What happens when a **sound** comes closer?

Answer on page 21

Did you know the answers? Give yourself a

Do you remember these **sound** words?
Well done! Can you remember any more?

noise
page 5

loud
page 6

quiet
page 7

high
page 8

low
page 9

voice
page 10

instrument
page 12

ears
page 17

listen
page 18

dance
page 22